DEVELOPED INDIA BY 2047

MY DREAM INDIA

PRAVIN RAMACHANDRAN NAIR

Made with ♥ on the Notion Press Platform
www.notionpress.com

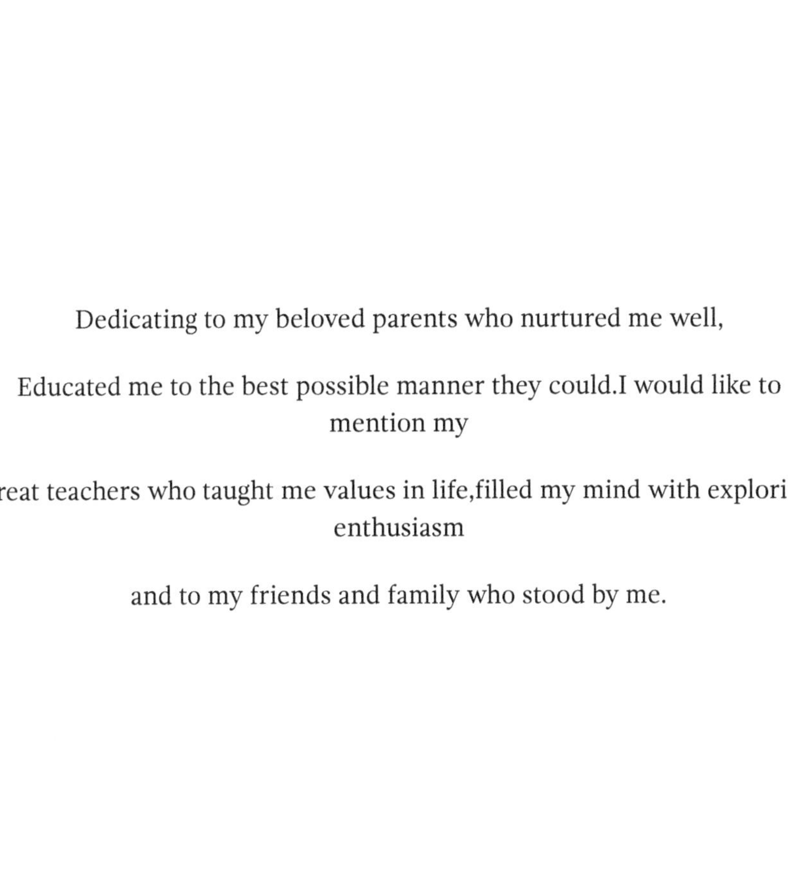

Dedicating to my beloved parents who nurtured me well,

Educated me to the best possible manner they could.I would like to mention my

great teachers who taught me values in life,filled my mind with exploring enthusiasm

and to my friends and family who stood by me.

Contents

Foreword

Started as a thought for a manifesto for the 2024 Parliament elections.

Noted down my thoughts and compiled this to a small book.

Foreseeing the great and revamped and advanced India ,where all her

sons and daughters are treated equally,where all of them have freedom of expression and

freedom of employment.There will be great celebrations,harmony and cultural exchange.

Thus threading the strings of diversity to a woven net of pure love and strong bond between them.

CHAPTER I

Developed India
by
2047

MANIFESTO
*EQUALITY*SECULARISM*RENAISSANCE

With 5 KEY Focus AREAS

Education

Employment

Entrepreneurship

Energy

E-governance

CHAPTER II

Education is the yardstick towards human empowerment--

EDUCATION

- FREE EDUCATION FOR ALL BY 2050
    - 3Y TO 17 YRS BPL STUDENTS (NO RELIGION/CASTE)

  * SLAB BASED GRANT FOR HIGHER INCOME GROUPS ?
- SAFE SCHOOLING FACILITIES WILL BE MADE MANDATORY
- SAFE SCHOOL TRANSPORT SYSTEMS SHALL BE IMPLEMENTED
- CAREER ORIENTED IT TRAINING COURSES TO BE INITIATED
- FACILITATE INTERNATIONALLY RECOGNISED COURSES

CHAPTER III

Decent livelyhood is the right of every citizen.....

EMPLOYMENT

- INCREASE THE JOBS IN PUBLIC/PRIVATE & JOINT SECTORS BY 30 % BY 2050
- KEY AREAS OF FOCUS

- SAFETY	- AGRICULTURE	- INDUSTRY SPECIFIC
- SECURITY	- FOOD PRODUCTION	- RAILWAYS
- SUSTAINABILITY	- FOOD PROCESSING	- PUBLIC TRANSPORT
-SOFTWARE	- AQUACULTURE	- CLEAN CITY

#Other Relevant Fields to be Analysed and Updated#

CHAPTER IV

Prompt ,monitored well regulated funding can bring in so many advancements in the country...

ENTREPRENEURSHIP

- PROMOTING STARTUPS
- SPECIAL SECURED FUNDS
- INVESTMENT INCUBATORS UNDER SUPERVISION
- ASSISTING IN INTELLECTUAL RIGHTS AND PATENTS
- PROMOTING RESEARCH AND DEVELOPMENT
- ASSISTING IN PITCHING IN TO VARIOUS MARKETS
- FAST TRACK APPLICATION PROCESSING

ENTREPRENEURSHIP

- PROMOTING STARTUPS
- SPECIAL SECURED FUNDS
- INVESTMENT INCUBATORS UNDER SUPERVISION
- ASSISTING IN INTELLECTUAL RIGHTS AND PATENTS
- PROMOTING RESEARCH AND DEVELOPMENT
- ASSISTING IN PITCHING IN TO VARIOUS MARKETS
- FAST TRACK APPLICATION PROCESSING

CHAPTER V

ENERGY

- 50% TOTAL ENERGY NEEDS FROM RENEWABLE BY 2040
- INCREASE SOLAR INSTALLATION
- DEVELOP CENTRAL RENEWABLE ENERGY COMPANY
- DEVELOP ADVANCED TRANSMISSION SYSTEM
- DEVELOP ADVANCED MONITORING SYSTEMS
- DEPLOY DOMESTIC AND INDUSTRIAL ENERGY SAVING SYSTEMS
- FORMULATE GREEN ENERGY SCORING SYSTEM
- DEVELOP 25 GREEN CITIES BY 2040

ENERGY

- DEPLOY ADVANCED ENERGY CAPTIVATION SYSTEMS
- DEVELOP CORPORATE SUSTAINABLE SCORING SYSTEM

  GS - Green Score - from *** TO ******* (3-7)

- ACCOMPLISH ENERGY EFFICIENT GOALS in OFFICES BY 2035
- ACCOMPLISH RENEWABLE ENERGY UTILISATION GOALS IN OFFICES

  50 % OF TOTAL FROM RENEWABLE SOURCES BY 2050

CHAPTER VI

E- GOVERNANCE

- ADVANCED DATA SAFETY SYSTEMS IN PUBLIC & PRIVATE SECTOR
- ENSURE DATA PRIVACY AND SECURITY
- DEVELOP A UNIFIED APPLICATION FOR ELECTRONIC LOGIN

  RURAL/DISTRICT/STATEWISE/NATIONAL LEVELS

E- GOVERNANCE

- DIGITALISATION OF GOVERNMENT OFFICES
- CLOUD BACKUP
- ENHANCED SAFETY MEASURES FOR E- GATEWAYS
- SINGLE PLATFORM AUTHORISATION OF LOCAL GOVERNMENT SERVICES
- SECURE ACCESS FOR SAFE AND SECURE ONLINE TRANSACTIONS
- PROMOTING ONLINE MONEY AND GOODS TRANSACTIONS

CHAPTER VII

GOALS

- INCLUSIVE DEVELOPMENT
- EFFECTIVE & MORALE EDUCATION FOR ALL
- EFFICIENT & RESPONSIBLE HEALTHCARE FOR ALL
- SAFETY FOR ALL - TRAVEL/EDUCATION/EMPLOYMENT/ENTERTAINMENT
- GLOBAL AGRO PRODUCTION HUBS
- GLOBAL FOOD PRODUCTION HUBS
- GLOBAL TECHNOLOGY PRODUCE HUBS
- ADVANCEMENT IN RENEWABLE ENERGY SOLUTIONS
- BECOMING A WORLD LEADER IN RENEWABLE ENERGY PROVIDER ROLE
- INCREASE EXPORTS
- INCREASE FDI WITH LIMITED ACCESS TO KEY AREAS

CHAPTER VIII

TASKS

- DATA SAFETY
- DATA COLLECTION
- DATA OUTREACH
- DATA SPEED
- DATA ANALYSIS

* SOLUTION
* PROVISIONING
* SELECTION OF PROVIDERS
* TRANSPARENT TENDERING
* TIME BOUND DELIVERY

CHAPTER IX

PROPOSALS

EMPLOYMENT

SECTORS

- HEALTH	- POLICE	- IT
- EDUCATION	- INTELLIGENCE	- OUTSOURCING
- TRANSPORTATION	- AVIATION	- LABOR SUPPLY
- MANUFACTURING	- MINING	- GEOLOGY
- FISHING	- METEOROLOGY	- HANDCRAFTS
- WHOLESALE AND RETAIL TRADE	- WAREHOUSING SOLUTIONS	- ENVIRONMENT PROTECTION

CHAPTER X

APPROACHES

- RETAIN THE GOVERNMENT SECTOR EMPLOYMENT
- TIMELY IMPROVISATION AND MODERNISATION
- PUBLIC PRIVATE PARTNERSHIPS
- MONETISATION OF GOVERNMENT COMPANY ASSETS

(NOT DISINVESTMENT)

- EFFECTIVE PLANNING OF PROJECTS
- FORESEEING THE FUTURE PITFALLS OF ANY PROJECT BEFORE APPROVALS
- RESPONSIBLE CONTRACTS FOR SAFETY/QUALITY/MAINTENANCE
- INCORPORATION OF MODERN TECHNOLOGY IN ALL SECTORS

CHAPTER XI

MAIN FINANCIAL TARGETS

- GROSS GDP/CAPITA - [illegible]000+ BY 205[illegible]
- CREATE NATIONAL JOB BANK
- CREATE 5 LAKH GOVERNMENT JOBS PER YEAR
- AIMS TO CREATE 5- 10 LAKH JOBS PER YEAR IN OTHER SECTORS
- INCREASE TAX REVENUE COLLECTION USING ADVANCED TECHNOLOGY
- BRING DOWN THE TAX EVASION TO LESS THAN 2.5% OF THE GST

CHAPTER XII

POLICY AIMS

- MOBILISING DOMESTIC WORK FORCE TOWARDS NATION BUILDING
- ENSURING JOB SAFETY AND FINANCIAL INDEPENDENCE TO WOMEN
- RE ANALYSE CIVIL LAWS IN PAR WITH INTERNATIONAL STANDARDS
- MODIFY/ADD/DELETE AS PER NEED OF THE TIME
- EVIDENCE BASED PRACTICE IN ALL PROFESSIONAL AREAS

  HEALTH/LAW/ENGINEERING/SCIENCE/RESEARCH

- POVERTY ERADICATION

CHAPTER XIII

REGULATORY CHANGES

CONSTRUCTION	MEDICAL PROFESSIONAL PRACTICE
INFRASTRUCTURE	LAW PROFESSIONAL PRACTICE
HEALTH	BANKING AND FINANCE
EDUCATION	ENVIRONMENT PROTECTION
AGRICULTURE	WAGES DETERMINATION AND DISTRIBUTION
DRIVING	PROTECTING VULNERABLE GROUPS

CHAPTER XIV

PROHIBITION OF NARCOTICS

- FORM SPECIAL TASK FORCE TO ACHIEVE 100 % DRUG/SMOKE FREE CAMPUSES
- FORM ZONAL DIVISIONS FOR SPECIAL ANTI NARCOTICS CELL
- DEVELOP MODERN DE ADDICTION CENTRES ACROSS COUNTRY
- FORMULATE WHISTLE BLOWER POLICY

This is just a few of the lot more goals to achieve.

In successive books I will try to narrate the details of the Key points discussed.

For all my brothers and sisters.......

www.ingramcontent.com/pod-product-compliance
Lightning Source LLC
LaVergne TN
LVHW070224170826

845679LV00033B/2222

* 9 7 9 8 8 9 4 9 8 5 6 6 4 *